FIRST GRADE
LEARNING MATHEMATICS FROM PICTURES TO WORDS

AUTHORS

DR. EDWARD C. HAYNIE

LAMAR HART

Table of Contents

Acknowledgements

This booklet is dedicated to Dr. Joyce Taylor Haynie for her interest, support, and belief in STEM (Science, Technology, Engineering, and Mathematics) and to Ethan Haynie who strongly encouraged the writing of this booklet. He believed that having strong skills in mathematics helped propel his career success in the field of Architecture.

Great appreciation is extended to Edward C. Haynie, Jr. for his marketing skills and to Jibri Robinson in recognition of his artistic skills in preparation of this booklet. Captain Patrick R. Haynie has been an inspiration while serving as an officer in the U.S. Marines.

Overview

This booklet presents a way for scholars to learn mathematical words from pictures. Word development is fundamentally used to improve reading, writing, mathematics, and science skills. We encourage all parents and teachers to emphasize learning in these areas for their young scholars. The pictures represent mathematical words that students need to know and understand to prepare for reading and completing word problems.

Goals for Mathematics in First Grade
- Enhance students' knowledge, understanding and skills related to Mathematics sight words.
- Help children to develop mathematic reasoning, skills, and enhance their ability to solve practical problems.
- Contribute to children's conceptual understanding of the world around them.
- Foster the development of positive attitudes in studying Mathematics.

First Grade
How Children Learn Mathematics From Pictures to Words.

Children learn Mathematics concepts from both the informal, unstructured experiments in their environment and the more formal, structured educational setting known as school.

The objectives of this booklet are to assist teachers understand how children learn basic mathematics skills and solve problems.

Learning Theories Applied to Mathematics for First Grade:

The Constructivists/Cognitive (Learning in action)
- Constructivists believe that children must be allowed to experiment physically with the things around them if they are to learn. They believe active learning builds mental structures.
- Jean Piaget:
  - Theory is age and stage related, which means that students go through definite developmental stages in their lives. Each stage must be completed before a person can attain the next stage.
  - Preoperational stage (2 years old – 6 years old) Acting on Reality
    - Children know that objects exist outside of themselves, recognize that objects have properties, and will use words to tell you so.
  - Concrete Operations Stage (6 years old – 12 years old) Action on Operations
    - Children will "operate" on objects by systematically filling containers back and forth; they will make statements that acknowledge the interrelatedness of the objects; will show that they understand how to reverse actions by filling and unfilling containers.

First Grade

The aim in Learning Mathematics From Pictures to Words is to build mathematics skills for First Grade students.
- Functions of Words
  - Read the word and draw a picture
- Basic Expressions
  - Dialogue with the correct pictures and complete a sentence.
- Making Short Sentences
  - Complete the sentences with the words from the pictures.

First Grade Common Core Standards

The First Grade common core standards provide students with a firm foundation while learning whole numbers, addition, and subtraction. As students progress, these standards prepare them for enhanced for learning and application of more demanding mathematics concepts and procedures.

Research supports the recommendation that efforts to enhance knowledge and skills in mathematics for First Grade should focus on the number core; learning how numbers correspond to quantities, and learning how to put numbers together and to take them apart (the beginning of addition and subtraction). These are complicated ideas that take time to learn. Research also suggests that without these critical building blocks in place, mathematics performance will suffer in later grades.

Operations and Algebraic Thinking

- Represent and solve problems involving addition and subtraction.
- Understand and apply properties of operations and the relationship between addition and subtraction.
- Add and subtract within 20.
- Work with addition and subtraction equations.

Number and Operations in Base Ten

- Extend the counting sequence.
- Understand place value.
- Use place value understanding and properties of operations to add and subtract.

Measurement and Data

- Measure lengths indirectly and by iterating length units.
- Tell and write time.
- Represent and interpret data.

Geometry

- Reason with shapes and their attributes.

Mathematical Practices

- Make sense of problems and persevere in solving them.
- Reason abstractly and quantitatively.
- Construct viable arguments and critique the reasoning of others.
- Model with mathematics.
- Use appropriate tools strategically.
- Attend to precision.
- Look for and make use of structure.
- Look for and express regularity in repeated reasoning.

Words to Know

1. 0 less than
2. 1 less
3. 1 less than
4. 1 more
5. 10 less
6. 10 more
7. 2 less than
8. Add
9. Addend
10. Addition sentence
11. Bar graph
12. Break apart a ten
13. Column
14. Compare
15. Cone
16. Corner
17. Cube
18. Cylinder
19. 19.Data
20. Difference
21. Digits
22. Double
23. Double plus 1
24. Doubles plus 2
25. Equal parts
26. Equal sign
27. Equal to
28. Estimate
29. Fact family
30. Flat surface
31. Four of
32. Fourth of
33. Fourths
34. Greater than
35. Greatest
36. Half hour
37. Order
38. Outside
39. Part
40. Picture graph
41. Plane shape
42. Plus sign
43. Pyramid
44. Quarters
45. Quarter of
46. Rectangular prism
47. Regroup
48. Related facts
49. Row
50. Same amount
51. Schedule
52. Shorter
53. Shortest
54. Side
55. Skip count
56. Solid figure
57. Sort
58. Sphere
59. Subtract
60. Subtraction Sentence
61. Sum
62. Take away
63. Taller
64. Tally marks
65. Tens
66. Trapezoid
67. Two of
68. Vertex (vertices)
69. Whole

Learning Mathematics from Pictures to Words

1. 0 less than

0 less than 8 is 8

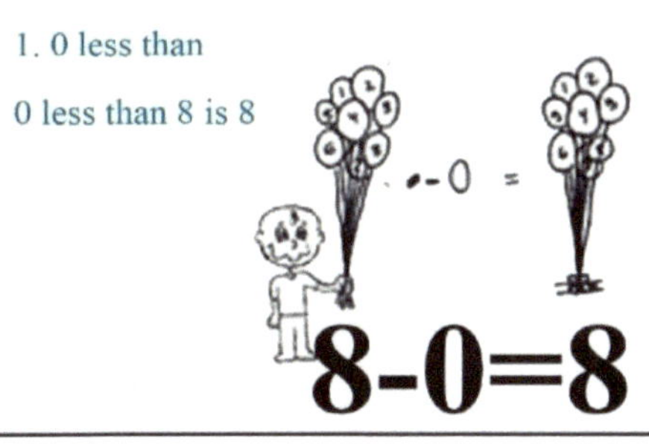

$8-0=8$

6. 10 more

10 more than a number has 1 more ten

2. 1 less

2 is 1 less than 3

7. 2 less than

2 less than 4 is 2

3. 1 less than

8. add

When you add, you find out how many there are in all.

$8-2=6$

4. 1 more

5 is 1 more than 4

9. addend

The numbers you add together to find the whole.

$5+6=11$

5. 10 less

10 is 10 less than 20

10. addition sentence

$1+2=3$

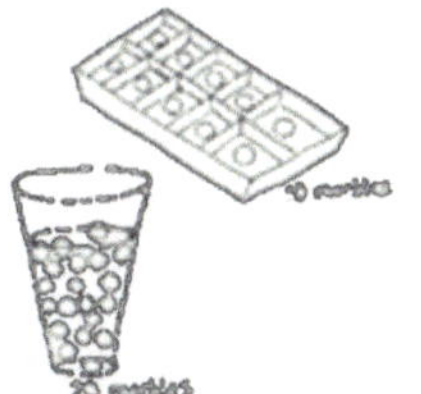

11. bar graph

A graph that uses bars to show data.

12. break apart a ten

Break apart a ten to make 10 more

13. column

14. compare

To find out how things are alike or different.

15. cone

16. corner

There are 8 corners on a cube.

17. cube

18. cylinder

19. data

The information you collect.

20. difference

The amount that is left after you subtract.

4-1=3

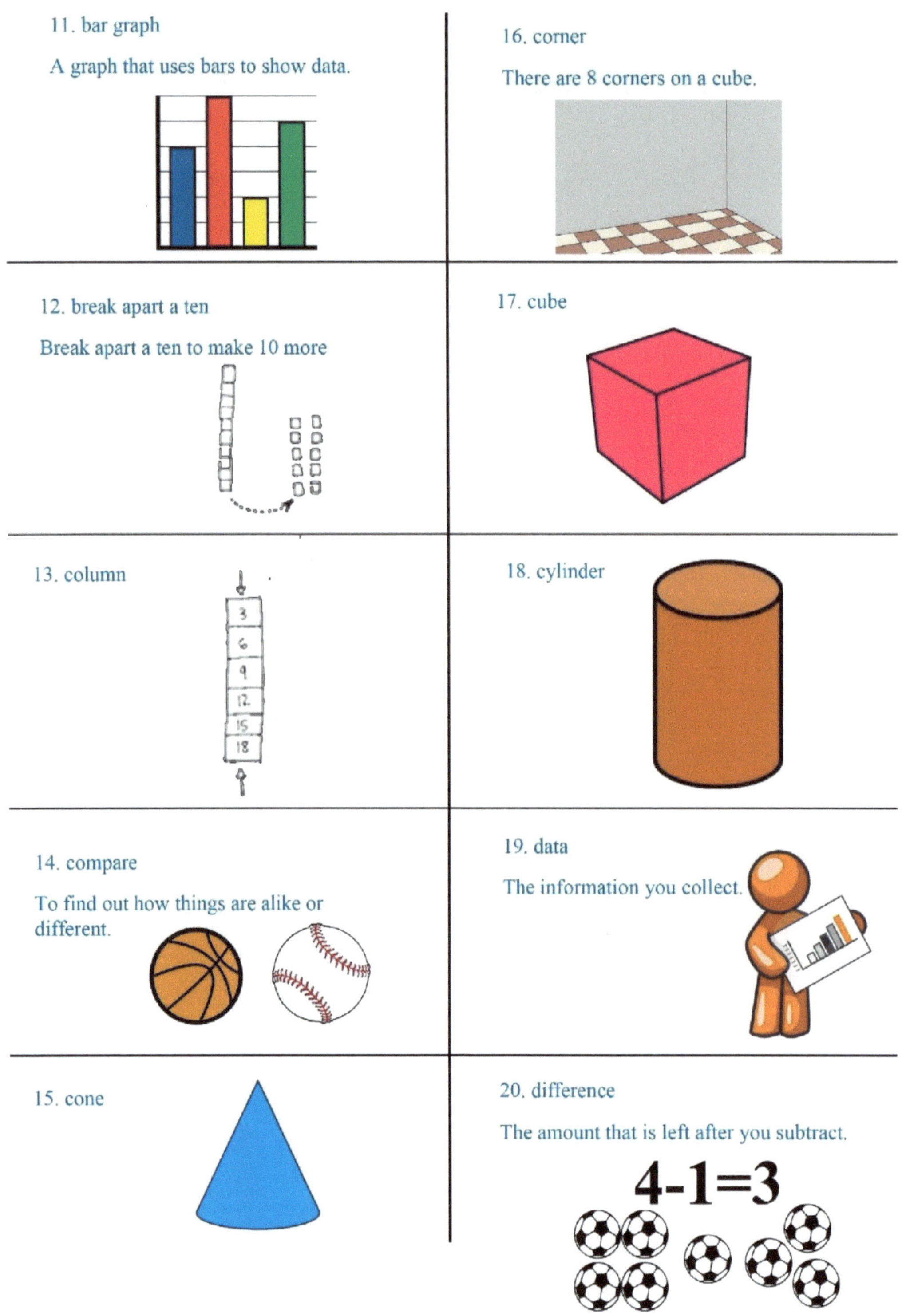

21. digits

Numbers have 1 or more digits.

2345689

26. equal sign

22. double

An addition fact with the same

4+4=8

27. equal to

6 + 3 is equal to 9.

6+3=9

23. double plus 1

A double plus 1 more with addends

8+8+1=17

28. estimate

24. double plus 2

A double plus 2 more with addends

9+9+2=20

29. fact family

A group of related addition and subtraction facts.

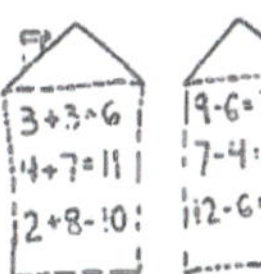

25. equal parts

Parts of a whole that are the same size.

30. flat surface

31. four of

Four of the quarters make one whole

36. half hour

A half hour is 30 minutes.

32. fourth of

A fourth of this square is shaded.

37. order

How one thing follows another.

33. fourths

Four equal parts of a whole.

38. outside

1 dog is playing outside of the house.

34. greater than

6 is greater than 4.

39. part

A piece of a whole.

35. greatest

The number or group with the largest

40. picture graph

A graph that uses pictures to show data.

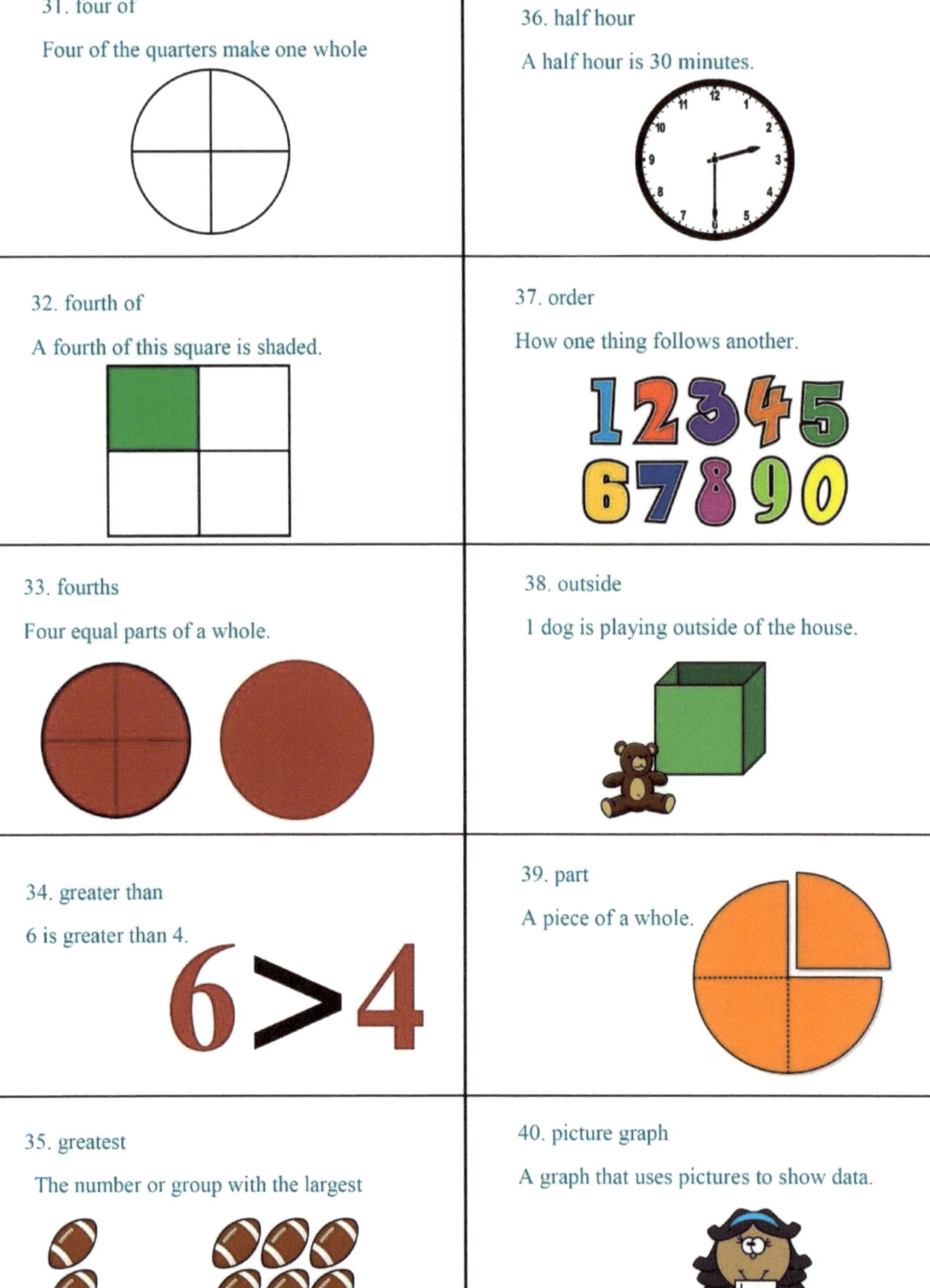

41. plane shape

A flat shape.

46. rectangular prism

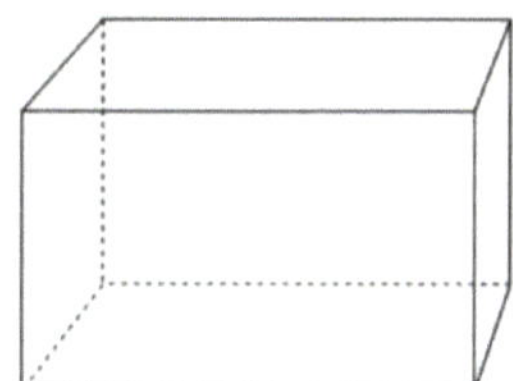

42. plus sign (+)

47. regroup

To make 10 ones into a ten or to break a ten apart.

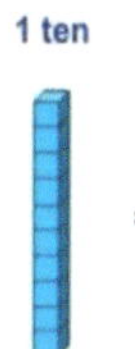

43. pyramid

48. related facts

Addition facts and subtraction facts that have the same number.

4+4=8
4-4=0

44. quarters

Four equal parts of a whole.

49. row

45. quarter of

You can describe one of the four equal

50. same amount

The same amount is on each side of the equal sign.

5=5

51. schedule

A list that shows what time events happen.

56. solid figure

A figure that has length, width and height.

52. shorter

57. sort

To group things according to how they are similar.

53. shortest

Least in length.

58. sphere

54. side

These shapes have straight sides.

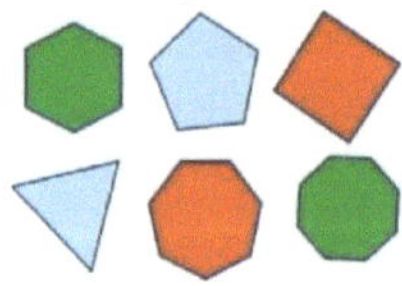

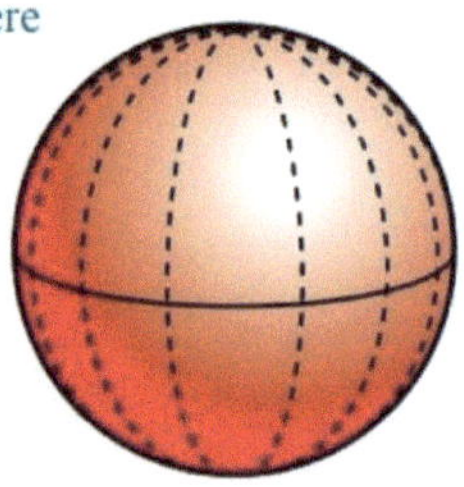

59. subtract

When you subtract, you find out how many are left, or which group has more.

5-3=2

55. skip count

You use patterns to count when you

5, 10, 15, 20

60. subtraction sentence

6-4=2

61. sum

$$19+5=24$$

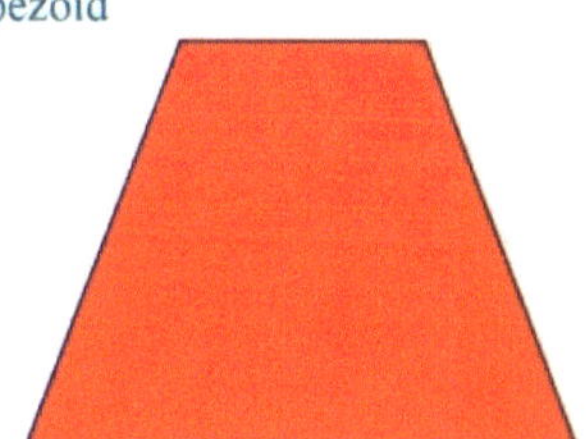

66. trapezoid

62. take away

To take away is to remove or subtract.

$$6-3=3$$

67. two of

Two of the halves make one whole.

63. taller

68. vertex (vertices)

A point where 3 or more edges meet.

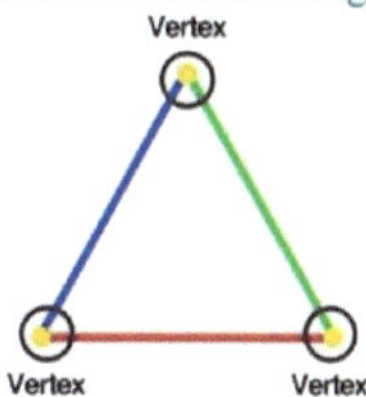

64. tally mark

Marks that are used to record data.

69. whole

You add parts to find the whole.

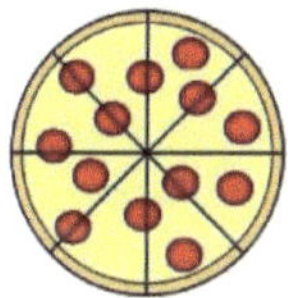

65. tens

The tens digit shows how many groups of 10 are in a number.

Blank Word Cards

The following pages have the pictures without the words. Use them to assess your scholar's knowledge of the sight words.

Suggested use:

- Print out the cards and use them as flash cards.

- Ask the scholar to identify what word(s) are represented by the picture.

8-0=8

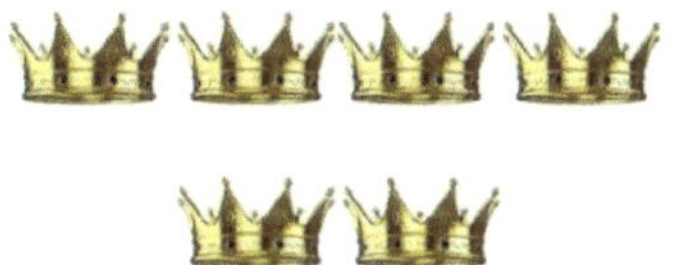

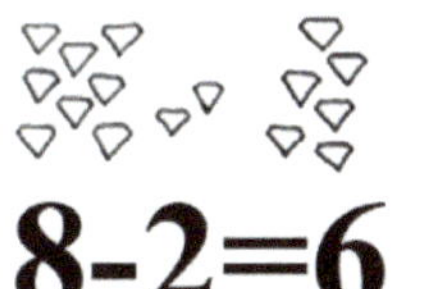

8-2=6

5+6=11

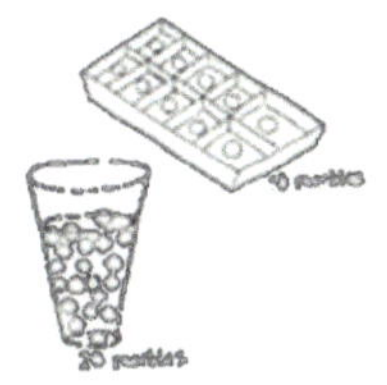

1+2=3

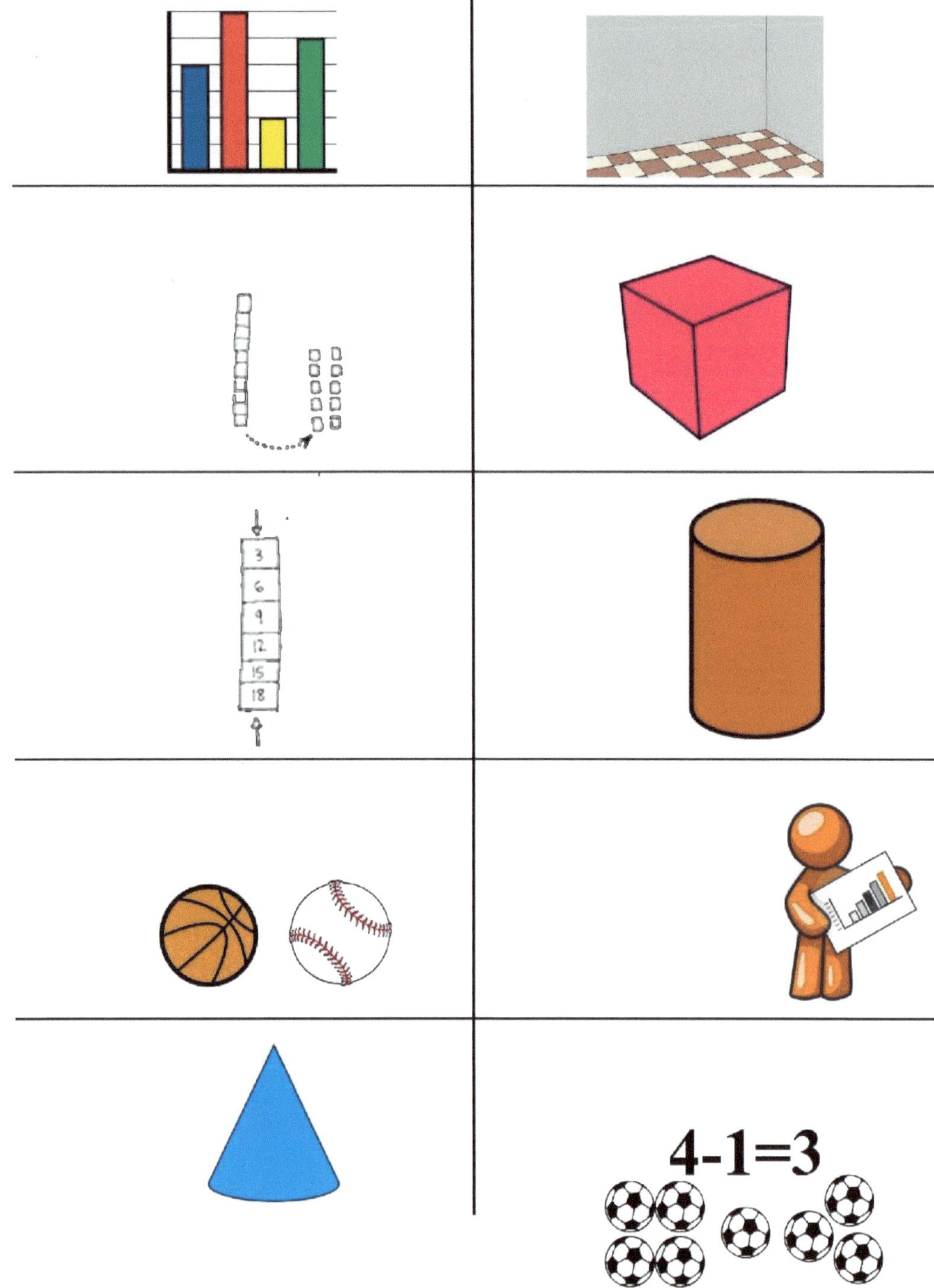

2345689

$4+4=8$

$6+3=9$

$8+8+1=17$

$9+9+2=20$

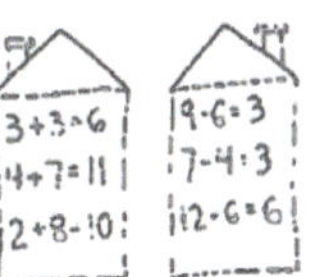

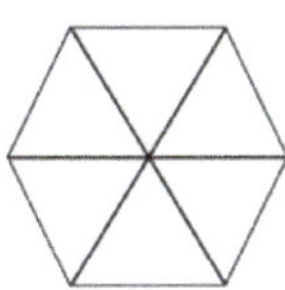

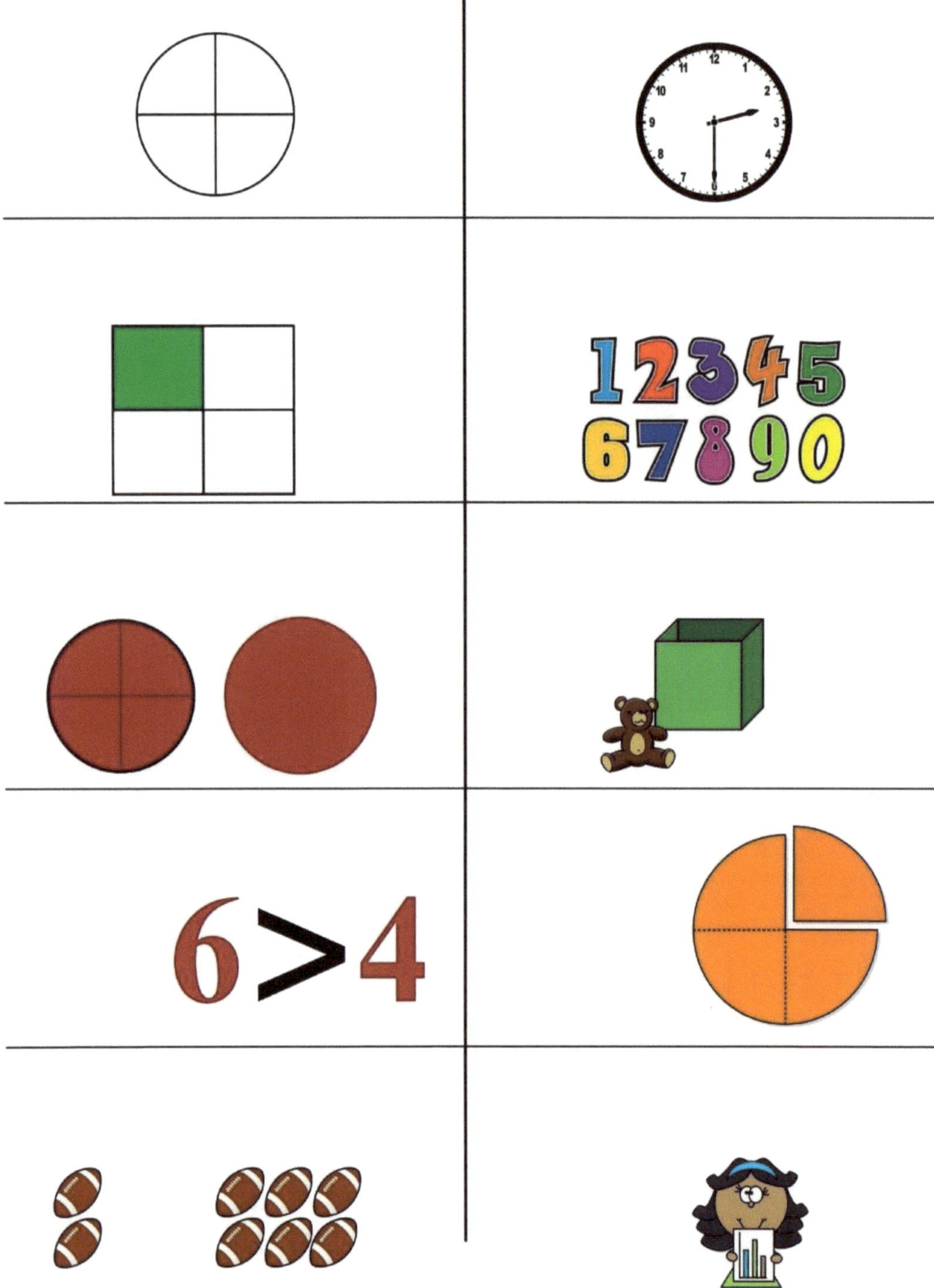

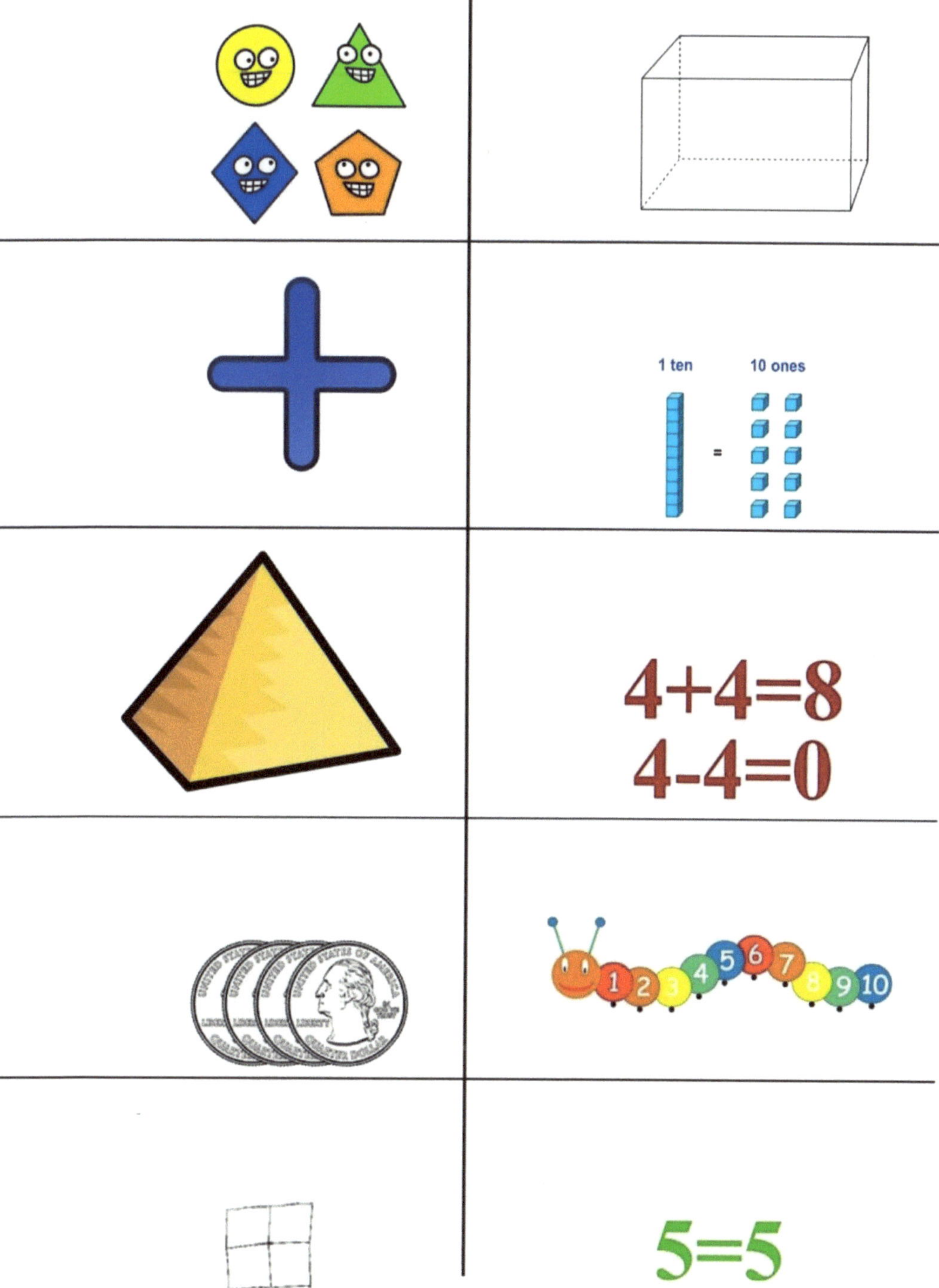

5, 10, 15, 20

5-3=2

6-4=2

19+5=24

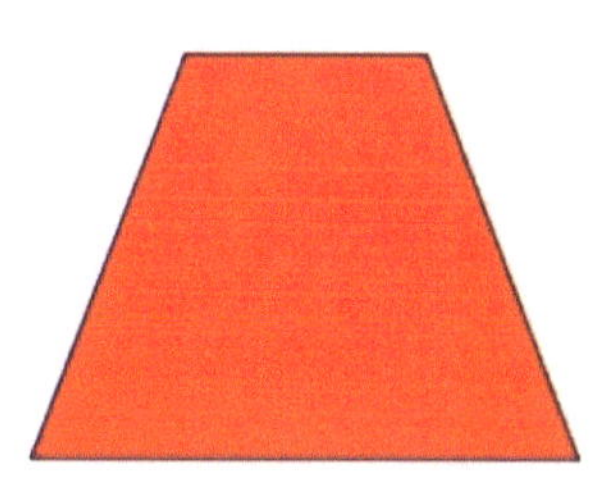

6-3=3

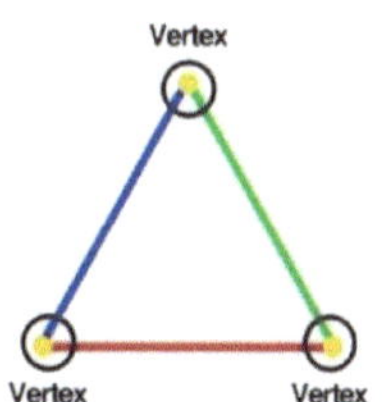

About the Authors

Dr. Edward C. Haynie holds a Bachelor of Science Degree in Chemistry and Mathematics, a Master of Science Degree in Chemistry, and a Doctor of Education Degree in Curriculum and Instruction/Science Education. Haynie has a vast and diverse background in science, which includes experiences in administration, teaching, research, planning, curriculum design and implementation of program in secondary schools, community college and university levels. He is also the Executive Director of the Incubator Scientist Program.

Lamar Hart received his Bachelor of Arts Degree in Computer Science with a minor in mathematics from Saint Louis University. He is a current student at Grand Canyon University, where he is finishing his Master of Education Degree in Early Childhood Education. He has worked in the field of education for over fifteen years as an Information Technology Director and Computer Science teacher, a teacher assistant at Barack Obama Elementary School. He has also worked with Dr. Haynie with the Incubator Scientist Program for the past ten years.